99 ½
Summer Jokes
with
Attitude

**Written and illustrated
by Holly Kowitt**

SCHOLASTIC INC.
NEW YORK   TORONTO   LONDON   AUCKLAND   SYDNEY

ISBN 0-590-21561-2

12   7 8 9/0

Printed in the U.S.A.   40
First Scholastic printing, June 1997

For Fisher Daniel

Special thanks to Joyce Pobursky

How Hot Is It?

It's so hot, even my shadow got sunburned!

It's so hot, the water sprinkler called in sick!

It's so hot, the sunflowers are wearing
Ray-Bans!

It's so hot, the Weather Channel is on the blink!

It's so hot, I saw Ren chasing Stimpy, and they were both walking!

It's so hot, my retainer melted!

Who did the Big Bad Wolf find at the tanning salon?

Little Red Riding Hood.

What do you call a hen who won't wear sunblock?

A fried chicken.

Why did the mother put cocoa butter on her little boy?

To stop son burn.

What happens when bananas sunbathe?

They start to peel.

How does a computer avoid sunburn?

It uses sunscreen.

Jock Itch

What does a surfer do when it rains?

Nothing. He's totally board.

What did one demolition-derby driver ask another?

"Can I crash at your place tonight?"

What happened to the janitor who took up surfing?

He wiped out.

What do you get when garbage collectors play basketball?

A pick-up game.

How does a monster congratulate someone?

He gives him a high six.

Why couldn't the mountain bike stand up on its own?

Because it was two-tired.

What does a Frisbee player do when he gets angry?

He throws a tantrum.

What kind of music do they play at the Olympics?

Heavy Medal.

When the brochure says: "Running water in every cabin..."

What they mean is: Big leaks over your bunk!

When the brochure says: "Sleep under the stars..."

What they mean is: Holes in all the tents!

When the brochure says: "See wild animals..."

What they mean is: Leeches, spiders, mice, and mosquitos!

When the brochure says: "Big lake free of jellyfish!"

What they mean is: The water is too polluted for them!

When the brochure says: "The food is terrific..."

What they mean is: As long as you don't eat it!

What Are You Doing This Summer?

Tie: Hanging around.

Videotape: Trying to unwind.

Thief: Taking things easy.

Stamp: Sticking close to home.

Tomato: Vegging out.

Jump rope: Skipping town.

You Go, Ghoul!

Why don't skeletons bungee jump?

They don't have the guts.

What vampire is young, yellow, and has an attitude?

Bat Simpson.

What kind of music does a witch bring to the beach?

A broom box.

What's a monster's favorite phone service?
Ghoul waiting.

What do undertakers watch on weekends?
Saturday mourning cartoons.

What do ghosts use to prevent sunburn?
Sunscream.

Why don't zombies bring sleeping bags to camp?

They don't sleep!

What did one ghost say to another?

"Get real!"

What do you call a funeral home that holds a summer sale?

A dead giveaway.

What do ghosts like to do on vacation?

Go white-water rafting.

What kind of music does the Invisible Man play?

Air guitar.

What Are Your Favorite Creepy Summer Reruns?

Slimefeld

Saturday Night Dead

NYPD Boo

Fiends

Gnome Improvement

Beverly Chills 90210

I'm just trying to finish my birdhouse, Mom. What— you think I'm in this for the POPSICLES?
POPSICLES
OPSICLES
POPSICLES
CLES
POPSICLES

Dressed To Chill

What kind of sneakers do giraffes wear?

High-tops.

Why did they throw the belt in jail?

It held up a pair of shorts.

Did you hear about the guy who fell in love with his blue jeans?

He wed his pants.

Why did the frog go to the mall?

To do his summer clothes hopping.

Why did the miniature golfer wear two hats?

In case he got a hole in one.

I'm Outta Here

Why did the sun worshipper take a vacation?

He was burned out.

Why did the bone doctor take a vacation?

He needed a break.

Why did the bungee jumper take a vacation?

He was at the end of his rope.

Buggin' Out

Why did the firefly ask to leave the room?

'Cause when you gotta glow, you gotta glow!

What do mosquitos give computer hackers?

Megabytes.

Why did the bee join the rock band?

To be the lead stinger.

What does a termite order at a restaurant?

A table for two.

What's a mosquito's favorite sport?

Skin-diving.

Did you hear about the bee with summer allergies?

He breaks out in hives!

Have You Ever Seen...?

a boat trip?

an ice cream shop?

a car phone?

a pizza stand?

a boardwalk?

Why did the camper leave his watch behind?

Because it was full of ticks!

What attracts shoppers to the Great Outdoors?

The mall of the wild.

Camper: Doctor, doctor, I think I have poison ivy!
Doctor: Try not to do anything rash!

Are We Having Fun Yet?

What kind of camp do janitors go to?

Sweep-away camp.

What's the difference between a camp lunch and an old pair of gym shorts?

In an emergency, you can always eat the shorts!

Camper: There's a spider on my burger!
Counselor: Hey—no pets in the mess hall!

What do you send a witch at camp?

A scare package.

Weather Is Here,
Wish You Were Beautiful!

What did you think of the big tornado?

I was blown away!

What do policemen do when they're hot?

They sweat bullets!

How do you buy a thundercloud?

With a rain check.

Hot Stuff

Why should you invite the sun to your party?

It knows how to break the ice.

What do you get when the sun goes surfing?

A heat wave.

What kind of car does the sun drive?

A hot rod.

What do you do if you're addicted to the sun?

Call a hotline.

How's Your Summer Job?

Good Humor man: Not so hot.

Weatherman: It's a breeze.

Coffee-bar waiter: I like the perks.

Aerobics teacher: It's working out.

Roller-coaster operator: It has its ups and downs.

How Did You Get Your Summer Job?

Puppeteer: I pulled some strings.

Ditch digger: I just fell into it.

Mechanic: I got a lucky brake.

Totally Iced!

What did the popsicle say to the Dove Bar?
  "Chill!"

What's pink, icy, and dangerous?
  A shark-infested Slushie.

Care to join me in a snow cone?
  Think we'll both fit?

How do you pay the Good Humor man?

In cold cash.

Why do you have a popsicle behind your ear?

Oh, no! I must have eaten my pencil!

What happens when burgers go on the Internet?

They get flamed.

What do rock stars like with their steak?

Moshed potatoes.

Why did the hamburger go to the gym?

It wanted better buns.

What did the mall rat take in summer school?

Buy-ology.

During the summer, where should a three-hundred-pound monster go?

On a diet.

Why did the traveler bring a hammer on vacation?

He wanted to hit the road.

Did you hear about the spoiled brat?

Last year he took a trip around the world. This summer he wants to go somewhere else!

What do you give the teller at a virtual bank?

A reality check.

Why did the moron tear a page out of his calendar?

He wanted to take a month off.

Summer Reading

Haven't Washed for Weeks
by Sandy Sheets

A Guide for Skinny-dippers
by Seymour Bottoms

Peeking into Beach Cabanas
by Sawyer Undies

Ants in My Bathing Suit
by Phil N. Jumpy

Throwing Water Balloons
by Mr. Again

Chilling Out

Why did King Arthur buy an air conditioner?
For those hot summer knights.

What did the lawn say to the sprinkler?
"Say it, don't spray it!"

What keeps a summer rock concert cool?
Thousands of fans!

Say Wet?

What kind of house does a lifeguard live in?

A real dive.

Did you hear about the private beach?

It's so exclusive, even the tide can't get in!

Where can you see lifeguards dance?

At a beach ball.

Why did the hacker buy a Boogie board?

He wanted to surf the Net.

What's an oyster's favorite rock band?

Pearl Jam.

Why did the swimmer get pulled over by a policeman?

He didn't have a diver's license!

How do lifeguards get to work in the morning?

They carpool.

Party Animals

What did the frog say on his answering machine?

"Leave a message at the sound of the peep!"

Why did the rabbit go on strike?

He wanted a better celery.

Why did the elephant get pulled over by a policeman?

For trunk driving.

What do you tell a pig who's going to the mall?

"Slop till you drop!"

Annoying Knock-Knocks

Knock-knock.
Who's there?
Canoe.
Canoe who?
Canoe row a boat in this polluted water?

Knock-knock.
Who's there?
Bugs spray.
Bugs spray who?
Bugs pray they won't get zapped!

Knock-knock.
Who's there?
Summer.
Summer who?
Summer stupid, some are not!

Letters from Camp

From diet camp: "This whole experience is wearing thin..."

From art camp: "I've been drawing lots of mosquitos..."

From gymnastics camp: "The counselors bend over backward for us..."

From music camp: "Just wanted to send you a note..."

From tennis camp: "My bunkmates are raising a racket!"

From fishing camp: "Why don't you drop me a line sometime?"

From computer camp: "My counselor told me to get with the program..."

SUMMER AWARDS

MOST HIDEOUS POPSICLE STICK CREATION

WORST SUMMER OUTFIT — BLACK SOCKS WITH SANDALS

MOST BOGUS SUMMER ALLERGIES
LIMA BEANS
CLEAN SHIRTS
YOUR SISTER

ATHLETIC AWARD for watching TV without the remote

THE LYIN' KING AWARD FOR CONVINCING YOUR MOM THAT CARAMEL CORN IS A SUMMER VEGETABLE

Wilderness Survival CERTIFICATE FOR HIKING WITHOUT A CELL PHONE

How Bad Were the Mosquitos?

They were so bad, even my socks got bitten!

They were so bad, the bug zapper wore bug spray!

They were so bad, the governor declared them the new state bird!

Did You Hear the One About...?

Did you hear the one about the camp with six-story cabins?

It's a lot of bunk!

Did you hear the one about the giant mosquito?

It's over your head!

Did you hear the one about the bed?

I just made it up!

Did you hear the one about the sun?

It's a hot one!

Did you hear the one about the frozen yogurt?

It left me cold!

What Did You (Really) Do This Summer?

I created music.

I worked on my pitching arm.

I was on the radio.

I practiced dribbling.

I exercised frequently.

I finally got rid of that bug
that's been going around.

Half Joke

What's black and white and red all over?

A _____ *that doesn't wear sunblock!*